MINIATURE HORSES

by Charlotte Wilcox

Reading Consultant

Sandy Tremont

American Miniature Horse Association

C A P S T O N E   P R E S S

M A N K A T O ,   M I N N E S O T A

C A P S T O N E   P R E S S

818 North Willow Street • Mankato, Minnesota 56001

Printed in the United States of America.

Library of Congress Cataloging-in-Publication Data
Wilcox, Charlotte.
   Miniature horses/by Charlotte Wilcox
   p. cm.--(Learning about horses)
   Includes bibliographical references (p. 45) and index.
   Summary: Discusses the breeds, characteristics, history, and uses of miniature horses.
   ISBN 1-56065-465-1
   1. Miniature horses--Juvenile literature. [1. Miniature horses. 2. Horses.]
I. Title. II. Series.
SF293.M56W54 1997
636.1--dc20

                                 96-42317
                                   CIP
                                   AC

Photo credits
William Muñoz, cover, 10, 22, 36
Visuals Unlimited/Mark Gibson, 6
Unicorn/A. Ramey, 12, 34, 42; Robert Ginn, 25; Gerry
   Schnieders, 32; Dennis Thompson, 38-39
FPG, 14
Al Jorolan, 16, 26
Cheryl Blair, 18, 30
Betty Crowell, 20
Julie Green, 29
Faith Uridel, 41

Table of Contents

Quick Facts about Miniature Horses

Description

Height:
Miniature horses stand 25 to 34 inches (63-1/2 to 86 centimeters) from the ground to the base of the last hairs of the mane.

Weight:
Minis weigh from 100 to 300 pounds (45 to 135 kilograms).

Physical features:
Minis have the same shape as a full-size horse, with long manes and tails and thick hooves.

Colors:
Minis come in every color a horse can be.

Development

History of breed:
Miniature horses developed over time. Breeders chose smaller and smaller horses over many generations.

Place of origin: Minis are bred separately in Europe, North America, and South America.

Numbers: More than 75,000 miniature horses are registered in North America. Their number doubles every five years.

Life History

Life span: A well-cared-for miniature horse may live 30 years or more.

Uses

Miniature horses are popular pets for people who would be unable to keep or handle a larger horse. They can pull carts and buggies and compete in sporting events. Only small children can ride miniature horses.

Chapter 1

What Are Miniature Horses?

Miniature horses are smaller versions of regular, full-size horses. They are often called minis. Minis can be almost any breed, but no one breed is always a mini. A horse is considered a miniature only if it meets the height requirements.

Horses are almost always measured in hands. One hand equals four inches (10 centimeters). But miniature horses are measured in inches or centimeters. These horses are measured from the ground to the base of the last hairs of the mane.

A horse is considered a miniature only if it meets the height requirements.

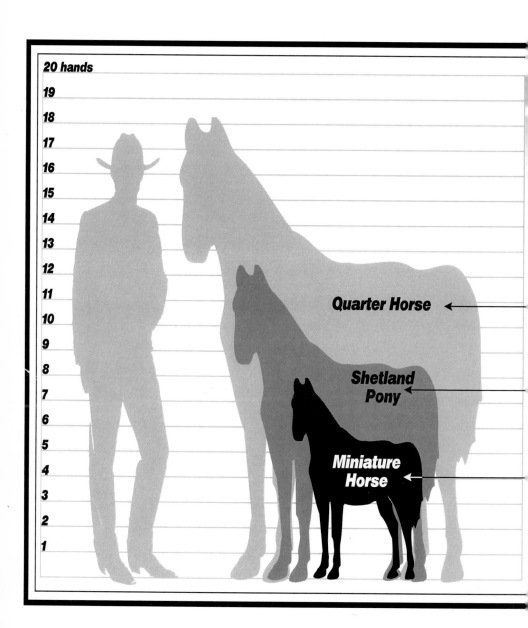

20 hands
19
18
17
16
15
14
13
12
11
10
9
8
7
6
5
4
3
2
1

Quarter Horse ←

Shetland
Pony ←

Miniature
Horse ←

Smaller Is Better

Miniature horses are less than half the size of a regular horse. Full-grown miniature horses stand from 25 to 34 inches (63-1/2 to 86 centimeters) tall. Breeders select the smallest stallions and mares for breeding. That way they hope to have even smaller foals the next year.

The American Miniature Horse Association does not allow young minis to be shown if they are too large for their age. Horses that are less than one year old cannot be taller than 30 inches (76 centimeters). Horses between one and two years old cannot be taller than 32 inches (81 centimeters). Two-year-old horses cannot be taller than 33 inches (84 centimeters).

Miniature horses weigh between 100 and 300 pounds (45 to 135 kilograms). An average-sized riding horse weighs 1,000 pounds (450 kilograms). A giant draft horse weighs about 2,000 pounds (900 kilograms).

A newborn mini weighs 18 to 22 pounds (eight to 10 kilograms). It stands 16 to 21 inches (40-1/2 to 53 centimeters) tall at birth. The smallest known miniature foal was only 12 inches (30-1/2 centimeters) tall when it was born. A newborn miniature horse is about the same size as a medium-sized dog, such as a Labrador.

A newborn miniature horse is about the same size as a medium-sized dog, such as a Labrador.

Chapter 2

The Beginnings of the Miniature Horse

Miniature horses have been around for at least 400 years. But no one knows where they first appeared. One story says that a herd of horses was trapped in a canyon. Because there was not much grass in the canyon, the mares started having smaller and smaller foals. The horses lived in the canyon for a long time.

Many years later, humans discovered the canyon. They found a herd of miniature horses. The horses looked just like their ancestors, but they were only half the size. This story is just a legend, but we do know that miniature horses came from larger horses. They are the result of careful breeding in Europe, North America, and South America.

Miniature horses are descended from full-size horses.

The Pets of Princes and Princesses

The earliest-known miniature horses came from Europe in the 1500s. They were pets in the palaces of kings and rich nobles. As the little horses became more popular, people tried to breed them smaller and smaller. Farmers bred the smallest horses and sold the foals to rich families.

A Law Against Miniatures

The small horses became so popular that King Henry VIII of England passed a law against breeding them. He feared that farmers would quit raising large horses. He was afraid that he would run out of horses big enough to carry soldiers in heavy armor.

The king ordered that all horses less than 56 inches (142 centimeters) tall be killed. But the English farmers loved their small horses. They refused to obey the law. Since that time, England has produced more small horses than any country in the world.

King Henry VIII of England passed a law against breeding miniature horses.

Chapter 3

The Development of the Miniature Horse

From the 1500s through the 1700s, miniature horses were usually considered very small ponies. They were not able to carry a rider or pull a heavy load. Only rich people could afford to keep a horse that could not do any useful work.

Ponies in the Coal Mines

In the 1800s, there was a huge demand for coal. Coal fueled the new factories, trains, steamships, and machines being built. Many coal mines opened in Europe and North America. They needed horses to pull loads of coal from the mines.

Miniature horses are not able to carry a rider or pull a heavy load.

Full-size horses were too tall for the tunnels. So thousands of small horses and ponies went to work in the mines. They were called pit ponies.

Many pit ponies spent their entire lives working in the mines. They even lived in underground stables. The ponies worked hard every day. The miners loved them and took good care of them.

When pit ponies grew too old to work, miners would often take them home as pets. Many ponies could not see well when they left the mines. Years of working in the dim tunnels made their eyes sensitive to sunlight.

Horse Traders and Pony Farms

In the 1900s, power equipment replaced ponies in the mines. Horse traders who had sold ponies to the mines no longer had a market. But some traders liked the tiny horses. They still kept a few around. Once in a while, someone would want to buy a small horse for a pet.

Power equipment eventually replaced minis working in mines. Still, people kept miniature horses as pets.

Norman Fields was a horse trader in Virginia. Fields started breeding the smallest horses he could find. By 1964, he had a herd of about 50 miniature horses on his farm. He found that people wanted to buy them.

A few years later, a pony trader named Smith McCoy found that he could earn the most money for his smallest horses. In 1956, he decided to raise only these tiny horses. He went across the United States searching for small horses. He bought only those that were less than 32 inches (81 centimeters) tall.

For about 10 years, McCoy bred these horses on his farm in West Virginia. When he put his herd up for sale in 1967, it was the largest herd of miniature horses in the world. Breeders from many cities came to buy McCoy's miniature horses. They started their own herds all across North America.

Miniature horse herds started to appear all across North America in the 1950s and 1960s.

Chapter 4

The Miniature Horse Today

Miniature horses became very popular. More and more people started breeding minis. Some people thought a registry should be started for miniature horses. A registry is an organization that keeps track of a particular horse breed.

American Miniature Horse Registry

In 1972, a group of miniature horse breeders met in Illinois. They started the first miniature registry. It was called the American Miniature Horse Registry. They started a list of pedigrees for miniature horses. A pedigree is a horse's family tree. The registry used records kept by some breeders going back to the 1940s.

Owners can register their miniature horses if the horses meet a height standard.

The American Miniature Horse Registry divides miniature horses into two divisions. Division A horses stand no more than 34 inches (86 centimeters) tall. Division B horses stand more than 34 inches (86 centimeters) tall but not more than 38 inches (96-1/2 centimeters) tall.

American Miniature Horse Association

The American Miniature Horse Association began in 1978 in Texas. It is now the largest miniature horse registry in North America. They register only miniature horses measuring not more than 34 inches (86 centimeters) tall. At first, they registered any horse that met the height standard. Then, in 1987, they closed the registry. They now only accept foals born to miniatures who are already registered.

The miniature horse grows more popular every year. In 1995, the number of minis registered was double the number in 1990. Every year more are added. There are miniature horse farms in almost every North American state and province, as well as in Brazil, Great Britain, Spain, Sweden, and Switzerland.

There are miniature horse farms in almost every state and province in North America.

Registering a Miniature Horse

The process for registering a miniature horse is different from the process of registering a full-size horse. Full-size horses are usually registered soon after they are born. Horses do not reach their full adult height for three to five years. Because height is the standard, minis have to wait to be registered. They must be three years old to be registered with the American Miniature Horse Registry. They must be five years old to be registered with the American Miniature Horse Association.

Young horses receive a temporary registration until they are old enough to be permanently registered. Then, if they do not grow too tall for the registration requirements, they receive their permanent registration at age three or five.

What Miniature Horses Look Like

Minis are small, but their shape, appearance, and personality are the same as any horse. Breeders try to produce a beautiful horse. They

Young miniature horses cannot be registered until they are at least three years old.

want minis to display the same power and attitude as a larger horse.

Miniatures come in every color a horse can be. They can be black, bay (reddish brown with black), sorrel (reddish brown), or palomino (golden). They can be solid colors, roans (mixed dark and light hairs), or pintos (with patches of white).

Miniature horses have especially long manes and tails. Their tails sometimes touch the ground. Their gentle personalities make them good pets for children, elderly people, and people with disabilities.

Big Differences

Miniatures are expensive to buy, but they are less expensive to keep than full-size horses. Miniature horses do not need as much room as full-size horses. They eat about one-tenth of what a full-size horse eats. A bale of hay would last a full-size horse a couple of days. It will feed a mini for a few weeks. A large backyard has enough grass to feed one miniature horse all summer.

Miniature horses come in every color a horse can be.

Owners must sometimes make changes in their pastures and horse barns to take care of minis. Because minis are so much smaller than other livestock, regular farm fences do not always work. A tiny miniature foal can walk right under a standard horse fence. Minis are also too short to eat grain from some standard-sized horse feed boxes. They are too short to drink from some standard horse watering tanks.

Because miniature horses are so much smaller than other livestock, regular farm fences do not always work.

Chapter 5

The Miniature Horse in Action

Miniature horses do not have very strong backs. They can only carry small amounts of weight. Because of this, only small children can ride minis. But these little animals still have strong muscles. They can learn to pull a buggy or cart.

Pulling Buggies

Miniature horses pull many families for quiet rides on country roads. But driving any horse on a cart takes training and experience. Many mini owners join carriage-driving clubs to learn the basics before they set out to drive their own horse.

Miniature horses can learn to pull a buggy or cart.

Even children can handle miniature horses well enough to compete in a show.

One miniature horse can easily pull two adults in a cart. The horses can also be hitched in teams of two, four, six, or even eight. Miniature horse teams can pull a larger buggy or a wagon with several people in it.

Special Tack

Miniature horses are much smaller than the horses that usually pull buggies. They need special tack that is just their size. Tack is the equipment that a horse wears while being handled or used. Tiny halters, harnesses, and bridles are made just for minis.

Buggies and carts are made with smaller wheels for minis. There are even special small horse trailers for hauling miniature horses. Some families just put them in the back of a pickup truck or van.

Showing a Mini

There are miniature horse shows all over North America. Miniature shows do not include riding events. Instead, handlers walk or run alongside their horses. People who do not have much experience with horses can take part. Even children can handle minis well enough to compete in a show.

Horses compete in many different events at shows. The special categories are called classes.

Halter Classes and Obstacle Events

A halter class is when the handler walks into the ring leading the horse on a rope. The horse is supposed to stand quietly but remain alert while the judges rate it. Judges rate a horse on its conformation. Conformation is a horse's shape and appearance. They also rate the horse on how well it stands in the show ring.

Obstacle course events are when the handler runs alongside the horse while it jumps over small railings and obstacles. In some events, the handler even jumps over the obstacles, too. Horses earn points for how many jumps they make without touching the railings with their hooves.

Driving and Roadster Events

There are also driving events for more experienced horse handlers. A driving class is when the horses are harnessed to carts or little buggies where the driver is seated. Driving classes are fun to watch because drivers dress up in fancy, old-fashioned outfits. There are classes for young people as well as adults.

There are many judged events for miniature horses.

Mane

Withers

Forelock

Knee

Loins

Hindquarters

Tail

Flank

Fetlock

The roadster event is especially exciting. In this event, miniature horses are hitched to racing carts. The drivers wear brightly colored costumes called racing silks. Drivers show their horses off at different speeds. The judge calls out when the entire group should change speed.

Miniatures at the Racetrack

One of the newest sports for miniature horses is harness racing. In harness racing, a horse is harnessed to a small racing cart. The driver sits on a seat in the cart. Full-size harness horses

Even adults can ride in carts pulled by miniature horses. Drivers need training to control the horse.

race on a mile-long (about a one-and-one-half-kilometer-long) track. But miniatures race only one-quarter of a mile (about half a kilometer).

Miniature harness racing began when a few miniature horse owners came together to race their horses just for fun. These informal events became so popular that in 1992, horse owners formed the International Miniature Trotting and Pacing Association. Now there are about 20 official miniature harness-race tracks in the

United States. Many states have their own miniature harness-racing clubs, too.

Discovering Minis

Some people never get to see a real horse close up. Miniature horses are solving this problem. They can go places full-size horses cannot.

Minis can walk into hospital wards, nursing homes, and school rooms. Miniature horses can cheer up sick children and elderly shut-ins who would never be able to visit a horse farm.

People with disabilities can also enjoy horsemanship with minis. They are easier to handle and care for, and they cost much less to keep than a full-size horse. A number of programs have started recently to introduce disabled people to miniature horses.

More and more people are discovering miniature horses and the things they can do. What was once an unusual animal has become its own special breed.

Miniature horses cheer up the sick and elderly people in nursing homes.

Words to Know

bay (BAY)—a reddish-brown horse with black legs, mane, and tail

bridle (BRYE-duhl)—a piece of headgear worn by a horse that controls it while riding or driving

conformation (kohn-fohr-MAY-shuhn)—the shape and physical characteristics of a horse

foal (FOHL)—a young horse

halter (HAWL-tur)—a piece of headgear worn by a horse used to lead it

harness (HAR-niss)—gear worn by a horse when pulling a cart or buggy

mare (MAIR)—a female horse

palomino (pal-uh-MEE-noh)—a golden horse with a silvery-white mane and tail

pinto (PIN-toh)—a horse or pony marked with patches of white and another color

roan (ROHN)—a horse of any solid color with white hairs mixed in

sorrel (SOR-uhl)—a reddish-brown horse with a light-colored mane and tail

stallion (STAL-yuhn)—a male horse

tack (TAK)—all the various equipment that a horse wears while being handled and used

To Learn More

Cooper, Barbara. *The Pony Club Book.*
Kenilworth, England: The Pony Club British
Equestrian Centre, 1995.

Edwards, Elwyn Hartley. *Encyclopedia of the
Horse.* New York: Dorling Kindersley, 1994.

Harris, Susan. *The United States Pony Club
Manual of Horsemanship: Basics for
Beginners.* New York: Howell Book House,
1994.

LaBonte, Gail. *The Miniature Horse.*
Minneapolis: Dillon Press, 1990.

Patent, Dorothy Hinshaw. *Miniature Horses.*
New York: Cobblehill Books/Dutton, 1991.

You can read articles about miniature horses
in *Discover Horses, Equus, Miniature Horse
News,* and *Miniature Horse World.*

Useful Addresses

American Miniature Horse Association
5601 South Interstate Highway 35W
Alvarado, TX 76009
E-mail address: amha@flash.net

American Miniature Horse Registry
P.O. Box 3415
Peoria, IL 61614

**International Miniature Trotting and Pacing
  Association**
575 Broadway
Hanover, PA 17331

Miniature Horse Rescue
P.O. Box 920
Fillmore, CA 93016

Western Canadian Miniature Horse Club
Rural Route 4
Calgary, AB T2M 4L4
Canada

Internet Sites

American Miniature Horse Association
http://www.minihorses.com/amha/

Horse Breeds
http://www.ansi.okstate.edu/breeds/horses/

Horse Online
http://www.horseonline.com/

Miniature Horse Galaxy
http://www.wave.net/SmallHorse/Paintbrush

Miniature Horses
http://www.powerhorse.com/josie/

Index